VIA Folios 18

THE COUNTRY OF ABSENCE

THE COUNTRY OF ABSENCE

POEMS AND AN ESSAY

FELIX STEFANILE

BORDIGHERA PRESS

Library of Congress Control Number: 2012937242

Printed in the United States.

Published by
BORDIGHERA PRESS
John D. Calandra Italian American Institute
25 W. 43rd Street, 17th Floor
New York, NY 10036

VIA Folios 18
ISBN 978-1-59954-045-0

OTHER BOOKS BY FELIX STEFANILE

POETRY

The Dance at St. Gabriel's
In That Far Country
East River Nocturne
A Fig Tree in America
The Patience that Befell
River Full of Craft

TRANSLATIONS

If I Were Fire: 34 Sonnets of Cecco Angiolieri
The Blue Moustache: Some Italian Futurist Poets
Umberta Saba: 31 Poems

ACKNOWLEDGMENTS

The poems listed here first appeared in the following publications, and are gratefully cited:

Approach: "Antonio Stefanile," "Letter from a Friend in Exile"
Differentia: "Farfalla"
Experiment: "Feast of San Gennaro"
Evansville Review: "Emily"
New Letters: "Andrew"
Poetry: "The Marionettes," "A Fig Tree in America," "Atlantis," "Poem for Selma"
Perspective: "Back Home in Indiana"
Poetry Broadside (NY): "How I Changed My Name, Felice"
Quicksilver: "The Day We Danced the Saint"
Sewanee Review: "Ballad of the War Bride"
Whelks Walk Review: "Carmen"

The translation of Umberto Saba's poem, "Ulisse," titled "Ulysses," first appeared in *Umberto Saba: 31 Poems* (Elizabeth Press), permission of Linuccia Saba. The Italian text is from Saba's collection, *Il canzoniere* (Mondadori). The Italian text of the sonnet by Cecco Angioglieri is from *Cecco Angioglieri*, ed. Gigi Cavalli (Rizzoli). The epigraph to Felix Stefanile's poem, "In That Far Country," is from a poem by Selma Stefanile, "I Know a Wise Bird," from *Sparrow Poverty Pamphlet* 42. The author's poem, "In That Far Country," is from his collection of the same title, *Sparrow Poverty Pamphlet* 43. The poems, "The Catch," "Soldiers and Their Girls," "Honorable Army Discharge," and "Taking Sides with John Ciardi," are from *The Dance at St. Gabriel's* (Story Line Press). "The Americanization of the Immigrant," "The Dance at St. Gabriel's," and "Tony" were first published in *From the Margin: Writings in Italian Americana*, eds. A. J. Tamburri et al. (Purdue University Press).

The excerpt from Felix Stefanile's condensed essay originally published in the *New York Times* under the title, "Confessions of an Editor," is gratefully acknowledged.

The excerpt from Felix Stefanile's essay, "American Is Still a Land of Searchers," originally published in the *Christian Science Monitor*, is gratefully acknowledged.

This book is dedicated to the mythmakers:

Aniello, Genoveffa, Francesco, and Selma

Those who live outside themselves live inside the expectations of others. — La Rochefoucauld, *Maxims*

If every picture I made was about Italian Americans, they'd say, "That's all he can do." I'm trying to stretch. — Martin Scorsese, *Premiere* (1991)

Robert Penn Warren used to say that a writer should feel about his country the way he feels about his mother: he loves her, but does not approve of all that she thinks and does. — Walter Sullivan, *Sewanee Review*

The hyphen is the Go-Between. — Felix Stefanile

TABLE OF CONTENTS

THE ALLEGORY OF THE HYPHEN

FELIX STEFANILE

I

My book, *The Country of Absence*, has a certain intrigue to it. I have chosen the poems — out of a much larger store — from work of mine that appears in previous volumes. The book, however, is not an attempt at a "selected poems" compilation. It is a gathering of some poems of mine, devoted to the Italian American experience, that lie scattered, in past collections among other material. It also contains new poems, and poems like "Farfalla" that are placed between bookcovers here for the first time, though they have been published in magazines. I leave it to the sages of intertextuality, whose fascinating scholarship plays a role in literary studies, to determine if what I now offer is a late bloom, or in its own right, a first book.

On January 22, 1992, my essay, "America Is Still a Land of Searchers," was published as the Opinion Page focus of the *Christian Science Monitor*. It was the first in a series of Opinion Page essays, by various hands, intended to reflect the cultural diversity in the hemisphere. My original title for the piece had been "Discovering Columbus," but that was the year the name Columbus was a dirty word, and the editors changed the heading. Somebody's heart was in the right place in the paper's Boston office, however, for the caption accompanying the new title reads: "A son of Italian immigrants found his own Columbus voyage, seeking the Other in the exploration of poetry." As an abstract this properly interpreted the theme I set forth in my essay.

A key passage of that brief memoir targets my experience during Story Hour, one Friday afternoon in 5B3, when Mr. Aronowitz, a teacher whom we adored, read from the poetry of Henry Wadsworth Longfellow:

> Because of him I cannot forget Longfellow's dark and lovely poem, "The Tide Rises, The Tide Falls." Longfellow's plangent language throbbed like a gong in my ears.
> For two or three minutes I let myself be surrounded by language as by a copious spirit, palpable, inescapable, and thrillingly alien. I became aware of how separated from my familiar world of broken English, street talk, and an Italian dialect I didn't always understand, this airy, melodious universe was. I felt as though I was stepping over a line somewhere, into undiscovered country. Loneliness welled up in me almost like homesickness. The aftershock of that reading stayed with me a long time. I had glimpsed the Other, without whom I could not be whole.

That undiscovered country was the country of absence, where my imagination had never been. I conclude the essay with a comparison of myself to Columbus, tracking the wilderness of my own heart, America as language. Longfellow made me a scribbler at ten years old. In a profound sense my moment of conviction, in an elementary school classroom, formed my life as a poet.

II

I emigrated to Newtown High School in September 1933. Two miles from my Italian neighborhood, the school in demographic terms, was a universe apart. A huge stone edifice, a block square, studded with turrets and a tower, and girdled by a tall, wrought iron fence, it was the landmark building of a solid middle-class community. Here you saw no outward traces of the Depression then raging in the country; no empty stores with soaped-over windows, no unemployed men chatting on corners, no garbage-strewn alleys — the result of reduced public service.

This shift in my context was brought forcefully "home" to me during first roll call. The names pelted around me like a cold rain: Ayers, Baynes, Coombes, Doughty, Lord, Morrison, Perkins, and so on. These were tribes of Other America. I wrapped my newfound shyness around me like a cloak against the weather. The sting was all the more pointed because we Italian Americans were a recent influx, caused by a school redistricting plan only put into operation a couple of years before. We were shunted, as a sizable minority, from our familiar jurisdiction, to a massively Anglocentric and Protestant arena. I felt my unlikeness like a blow.

The occasional racial slur I endured, or overheard, I absorbed with the dogged patience of a boy constantly being warned by his elders to be "nice." You must remember that in the Thirties social struggle took place primarily in the labor movement, not in racial identity coalitions. What I felt were the distinctions of class all around me. The tribes of Other America, unlike me, came to school in suits. Their chat, as I eavesdropped in the lunch room from my always "separate" table, was about week-end tennis matches, tea dances, even croquet on the lawn. To an adolescent from my side of the railroad tracks dividing my neighborhood from theirs, these were important concerns.

Fate delivered me from my isolation through a chain of events I could not have foreseen. Towards the close of my first school year the Mayor's office issued a directive to high school officials to devise a city-wide homework assignment for all English grades: it would consist of an essay on fire prevention. The assignment was to be treated as a competition, with winning entries to be selected, and awards to be conferred. In the spring of 1935 the principal's office, through my English teacher, informed me that I was the recipient of first prize for sophomores. *The Newtown X-Ray,* our school paper, dubbed me "the sophomore of the ages."

About a week later an editor of the paper tracked me down during study period in the auditorium. She was a senior, a rank that at my age imposed attention, and asked me to "write something" for the *X-Ray.* In my beleaguered state of mind this was an invitation that had quasi-official overtones. I pleaded inexperience, but she stood her ground, and I agreed to do my best.

The piece I wrote was an appeal to Newtown to join the "national effort" to prevent Walt Whitman's house in Huntington, Long Island, from being sold to a commercial group interested in converting that "hallowed site" into a road-house. I gave the name and address of the Defense Fund organized to raise money to outbid the dastardly "money-changers," and preserve "this shrine of American letters." My prose, in plain truth, was a précis of a story I had read some weeks before in the *New York Times,* but the cry to heaven was mine. To the joy of the *X-Ray's* editors — and my own embarrassment mixed with pride — my call to arms attracted several donations from outraged parents, teachers, and other defenders of the faith. The school authorities were delighted to forward the money to the Defense Fund. Months later the Whitman home was rescued, and we all took our share of the credit for it in the *X-Ray.*

Such a flurry of excitement did not elevate me to star status at Newtown. That role, among Italian American pupils, was reserved for Joe Spagna, our famed home run hitter on the excellent baseball team the school fielded that year. But it did open some doors for me. The faculty sponsor of the Garretson Scribes, the school's poetry club, so named for a wealthy donor family that maintained the group in high style, with resources for guest lecturers, poetry "soirees," and other cultural affairs, sought me out and asked me to become a member.

My experience in the Garretson Scribes became the high point of my life at Newtown. For the first time, and in a relatively unconfined setting, I had the opportunity to move in a social milieu that reflected Other America. As you can imagine, the organization was filled with Doughtys and Perkinses, and I had to learn to control my shyness among them. I also profited, hearing my poetry discussed by my peers, from the guidance of a gifted mentor. Frances Butterfield, the faculty sponsor, was a poet herself, and an ebullient Muse, a person whom today we would call an activist. Newtown could not hold her, and in time she went on to become a key functionary on the Board of Education, where, among other duties, she directed the New York City annual high school poetry contest and festival, a well-known event that was invariably covered in the newspapers. She loved poetry, and that love and excitement radiated towards the dreamy adolescents in her charge. She made us feel not only privileged, but responsible. She ran the best poetry writing class I have ever come across, and she did not do so — as teachers seem to do today — by telling us how wonderful we were, but how wonderful poetry was.

III

I date my coming of age as a poet to 1950 when, for the first time, work of mine appeared in *Poetry*. Karl Shapiro, then editor of the magazine, accepted two poems. In that post-World War II decade, *Poetry* was the most renowned verse journal in the English-speaking world, and, for poets, the publication towards which all critical scrutiny turned. A first appearance in its pages took on the nature of a debut before the peerage.

I include one of the two poems, "The Marionettes," in *The Country of Absence*. I cite it because the poem was my declaration, before a key segment of the American reading public, of my unlikeness. The author of "The Marionettes" was not the crestfallen lad of seventeen years before who, in Newtown High School, had felt his unlikeness like a blow. It was my hope that the relentless Italian foregrounding and referentiality of the work would bring a new note to the well-established literary theme of the conflict between Art and Life. We may be sure that Oscar Wilde, when offering his witticism about Life imitating Art, did not have my emphasis on Pinocchio, Master Gepetto, Colombina, and "the barking of Melampo" in mind.

I drank from the well of small victories, and was refreshed. Poetry, the continuum that bridged the gap between the opposing poles of my dual nature as an Italian American, became my hyphen. I had celebrated, in a public manner and on my own terms, the marriage of my American North to my Italian South. My sense of self-verification was immense, and spurred me on.

In 1954 Selma and I issued the first number of a verse journal, *Sparrow*. To give the flavor of this Mom-and-Pop grocery-store operation, let me serve an excerpt from an essay of mine, "Confessions of an Editor," that was published in Bill Henderson's Pushcart Press volume, *The Art of Literary Publishing* (1979). It was reprinted, in a 3,000-word condensed version, in the *New York Times Book Review* of February 17, 1980:

> I have never deluded myself as to the importance of *Sparrow*. I have never wanted to compete with Random House or Doubleday. For philosophical reasons I shall go into later I believe such a fanciful contest is absurd to contemplate and foolish to propose. And I have never thought of poetry publishing as an ideological crusade or a revolution. My motivation for entering the field was, in truth, quite personal and selfish. I wanted to live the life of poetry.

This brief outline of my not so sentimental *education sentimentale* as a budding poet would not be compete without some account of "How I changed my name, Felice," which I wrote in 1958. Here, it seems to me, the thesis and antithesis of the hyphen I have striven so mightily to identify in "The Marionettes" behaves much like a metaphor. The synthesis is the line "Felix was American for me." A fitting off-spring of the collision-and-embrace of Italian and American. Is this a poetics of citizenship taking place?

IV

I want to say something about the canon now, a three-dollar word so fashionable among sociologues, ever-piping in our midst, that it is in danger of becoming pure jargon. I shall do so by discussing Emily Dickinson and the Rap poets in the same breath. Emily Dickinson, a powerful literary icon of the latter half of the twentieth century, was the most marginalized poet in American letters. Unlikeness was her fate, despite her impeccable Puritan genealogy as a member of a family prominent and well-connected in the New England society of her time. The Dickinsons were leaders in the local politics of Amherst, a university town with pretensions.

The story of Emily Dickinson, "the nun of Amherst," is too familiar to need elucidation from me. She has captured the American imagination for her mysterious life of seclusion and the taut, electric probing of her tireless spirit that registered its turmoil through poetry. Her popularity — she died in 1886 — remains the Consternation of the Correct. The simple truth is that though she wrote close to 1,800 poems only ten saw publication in her lifetime.

Emily Dickinson was not published because she would not write like a lady. According to the "two spheres" dictum of Victorian America the literary worlds of male and female poets were prescribed by the public authority of taste and decorum — which is what the canon is. This authority demanded of women a verse that was genteel, domestic, of limited scope, and as well-behaved as a caged bird. Passion was permitted in the magazines and newspapers only under certain rules; the passion was to be unrequited, or doomed, or, preferably, quelled by moral resistance.

The record is also clear that Emily Dickinson *knew* editors and poets, enough of them to make a networking MFA graduate of the present day turn green with envy. Had she complied with courteous requests to revise her creative temperament, and shape her work to pass muster in the general taste of the period, she would have been published more widely. She remained, instead, a poet censored by omission. The etiquette of her spry and sly refusals to mend her literary ways — her correspondence with would-be mentors is fascinating reading — unmask not the poet, but the canon that smothered her career.

Today the poems of Emily Dickinson speak to a vast audience, her readership is international and loyal. The authority that silenced her is a dead letter. In her mind-boggling innocence of purpose the poet's fame gives the lie, also, to a reigning shibboleth of our own era, that "Literature is Power." In Emily Dickinson's case literature was *powerlessness*. I try to give my response to this gorgeous paradox in the poem "Emily," included in *The Country of Absence*.

There are two inferences to be drawn here. The first is that the canon, for all its force, only endures when society obeys it. When, after her death, the poetry of Emily Dickinson began to be issued in a series of cautiously edited volumes, a surprised public reacted favorably — one of the books went into six printings, I believe — and the red-faced canon of Emily Dickinson's despair started its long retreat. In terms of genuine down-to-earth history, the canon is a fiction that is agreed upon. Disagreement kills it.

The second inference is that the literature of powerlessness exists, and always has. The far-flung past is filled with Emily Dickinsons, John Clares, John Keatses, to mention a selected few from the splendid tradition of the English lyric. Other nations can boast the same phenomenon. In Italy, the slender legacy of three sonnets ascribed to a medieval author identified only as *La Compiuta Donzella* (the accomplished maid) incited debate among scholars. No doubt driven by sexist impulses these offer explanations centering around a male author hiding himself behind an assumed anonymity. Other examples could be served.

A century after the verse of Emily Dickinson was first issued in book form, powerlessness, metamorphosed into its own authority, was once more demonstrated in the rise of Rap poetry. The art of a youth culture sprung from the ghetto, its success — now the mighty darling of the music industry — was as unexpected as that of Emily Dickinson, and as prevailing. Its influence on contemporary writing, especially poetry, cannot be denied. It is being offered as a workshop discipline at writer's conferences, always a sure sign of arrival.

Despite obvious differences, the kinship between these two modes of poetry is compelling. Most significantly, each comes to us unbrokered, in no way mediated by the canon. These poets are self-credentialed. Each mode springs from the same source, the inexhaustible mother lode of English lyric, the Common Measure. They are children of the ballad, with its roots reaching down six hundred years. In Emily Dickinson the lore stems more particularly from the hymn, the late, and refined child of the ballad. Yet her craft retains the pristine directness and simplicity — on most occasions — of the older rhythm, the four-and-three beat of the alternating lines, and the abcb rhyme pattern.

Rap, instead, finds itself at home in the "unwritten" tradition of "Sir Patrick Spens" or "The Wife of Usher's Well," with a tendency to be broad in its hints, bold in its humor and anger, and less regardful of the niceties Emily Dickinson is prompt to observe. Rap boasts and swaggers; Emily squeals, and calls a snake *a narrow fellow in the grass*. Both modes, however, visit sorrow and death and love regularly, and with the passion of the anonymous legends of unwritten tradition. In this sense each mode creates, stunningly sometimes, not symbol but myth, the eternal verity practiced over and over. Emily Dickinson's "I dreaded that first Robin so" (348, Johnson), which anticipates T. S. Eliot's opening lines from "The Wasteland" (*April is the cruelest month*), portrays a marauding New England spring with a cinematic sweep of flooding immediacy. I give the first two stanzas:

> I dreaded that first Robin so,
> But He is mastered now,
> I'm some accustomed to Him grown,
> He hurts a little, though —
>
> I thought if I could only live
> Till His first Shout got by —
> Not all Pianos in the Woods
> Had power to mangle me —
> . . .

Rap does not offer this, but has its own Orphic swell, the brio of the vocal delivery set against a musical background of tremendous pressure. The new "note" of video brings to performance poetry an added dimension.

V

I have chosen Emily Dickinson and Rap as my paradigm because their impact on us is beyond dispute, and because though one hundred years separate them, they remain partners in the crime of canon-breaking, especially as their unlikenesses intersect in the ballad. This factor of the ballad is, in the end, an aspect of language.

The mystery of language is the workshop of most hyphenated Americans, bereft as they are of the genealogical protocols of managerial America. To them, coming as they do from marginalized communities, the vocabulary of acculturation presents hazards beyond those of mere ambition. For their poets, the result is a process of hyperattentiveness resembling compulsion. No one studies as hard as the self-taught; overcompensation becomes gymnastic and heartfelt. Above all, they must learn to take an audience for granted where no audience may exist because they are constructing their own contexts. The discipline is not for sissies.

I have privileged the ballad only to delineate the paradigm. In simple truth all of managerial America is "unwritten tradition" to hyphenated writers. This gives them — I am thinking of figures like Pietro Di Donato, Langston Hughes, William Saroyan, Richard Wright — the energy of their recency. They deliver not only literature, but news, the political act of their new-fangledness. Or, masters as they are of the art of over-compensation, they become, like John Ciardi or Alfred Kazin, dons of the national discourse while at the same time not abandoning the immigrant heritage. Who gave us a permanently inimitable translation of Dante's *Comedia*? John Ciardi. Who wrote a great classic — the account of a dreamy boy living in the Jewish Brooklyn of yesteryear — *A Walker in the City*? Alfred Kazin.

My poem "Hubie" springs from a loyal memory of World War II, when African Americans were being admitted, like test-runs, into White military units. This practice began about five years before President Truman's famous Executive

Order of 1948. I try to depict the moves toward friendship of a Black Soldier, and a White Soldier.

I wanted the technique of the poem, its gears, so to speak, to propel in some iconic manner the conflict expressed in the poem's language. I have always had a fondness for friction in poetry, the way the poem fights with itself. There is as much "superstition" in this predilection of mine, which I yield to now and then, as logic, but that's how poets are. As Plato says, poets know no shame, and are not to be trusted. After several erratic starts, I decided on the rhymed couplet as my way of "driving" my point home. The couplet is spry, and amenable to emphasis. It also travels well in narrative.

By some lucky chance I recall, at almost the same moment of this decision, a canard about the rhymed couplet, the closed couplet in particular, circulated by a deconstructionist of yore. The deconstructionist stated — I am paraphrasing here, but I make my meaning plain — that the rhymed couplet exemplified in the witty, controlled verse of Alexander Pope reflected faithfully the rationality, stability, and economic control of the mercantile, imperial England of the eighteenth century. You must recognize here our old friend, "Literature is Power." I have always harbored a resentment of that theory because it besmirches my dream of language, and my respect for its mystery.

The upshot of all this is that I composed "Hubie" in what I think of as "fractured" couplets, unstable, occasionally irrational and never imperial. The couplets are closed, open, off-rhymed as well as rhymed, and the scansion of the lines is — not infrequently — impolite. The speaker of the poem, and "Hubie," are not polite characters. They are innocent, ignorant, and lost. If the poem succeeds for the reader it will do so through struggle towards some urgent truth.

I have avoided using the master-term hegemony in my comments on the canon. The actual power to "control" that hegemony signifies is ambivalently applied these days. As we are all aware there have been, for years now, efforts by federal and state governments to encourage and foster "diversity" in the schools. Philanthropic organizations, some of them quite huge, are geared toward supporting social amelioration of this kind. The temper of the times seems to indicate that a strong majority of Americans favor a national project recognizing and assisting the unrecognized and the unassisted of our marginalized communities. Unfortunately, especially in the area of cultural support — that is to say, money for the arts — these programs are racked by debates out of all proportion to the issues involved. The results of our vast national activity are still unclear.

I prefer to keep to my idea of language as the Canon behind all canons. This is something poets can understand. I conclude by appealing to young poets, assailed by thoughts of their own unlikeness, to take heart: the country of absence, where the imagination has never been, is a land where Possibility grows, like a peach in the sun.

THE COUNTRY OF ABSENCE

THE CATCH

Your college learn you be smart, talk fancy. You go with the girls, talk fancy. You tell your mother, Ma, why you got the bun on your head, old fashion. Your college learn you don't respect your mother. Some college. Now you say this girl you live together, marriage never mind, old fashion. Your mother cry, and with the beads, pray, pray, and pray. What you think, she ask me. You know what I think, boy? I think if you was pig we raise by and by we sell you for money now, not your mother cry.

TONY

Tall,
smiling-faced immigrant,
at school your handsome snickering
obsessed the rest of us.

The windows,
barred, as in prison,
looked down and gleamed at you,
which made us mad to follow
in the wake of your little scandals.
Our kind teacher
talked over our heads to you.

I remember
bouts of snobbery
when I schemed like a gambler
over my homework,
and rolled my eyes in class
at your inexorable ignorance.
Alert as a mouse
I used to loiter in the hallway
to hear
the useless reprimands
you received after class.
I scampered home,
thrilled with your shame.

Across the aisle
I ogled you like a girl.
I envied you your wild curls,
hair, that like you,
refused to stay in place.

I think I pitied you,
the holes in your shoes.

How brave,
how uselessly brave, Tony,
to dare your banishment.
What a scene at thirteen years,
you, chiding the Cyclops
to find you out.
Recalling that
plagues me now
like something choked down —
we laughed, we stamped our feet,
we hooted the principal
at her harangue,
the teacher, tears in his eyes,
who escorted you down the hall
like a jail-house priest.

Destiny, Destiny,
why were you so pretty,
so sure to die?

Before the summer was out,
and the grass dead,
you were struck down
as by a thunderbolt.

You were caught in a stolen car,
yourself the darting child you didn't see,
and iron rang in your ears.

Years later I saw you on Tenth Street,
pushing your wagon-load of fruit.
The sun seized you
like a searchlight
in our little square,
where you peddled your wares

in a brutal tremelo,
hoarse, out of breath.
Smiling-faced,
I stood before you,
blocking your way.
But you pushed around,
you stared right through me,
like a prisoner at Auschwitz,
seeing nothing but his death.

FEAST OF SAN GENNARO

And I remember figs strung on a wall,
and peppers, red and vicious, in a bowl
with thyme and fennel, on the window sill
beyond my reach, who wasn't very tall —

and sunlight spilling into the tiny room
to fall like plunder at my mother's feet
while at the table, calmly, calmly, she beat
the dough as if it were a golden drum —

and father's silly knocking at the door,
singing that Lola was his lady-love,
and chestnuts in my pockets, round and warm,
and Uncle Tony snoring by the stove —

and my fat cousins in their squeaky shoes
I can recall, and the quick, sudden pride
of my own laughter, and the wine, and how
tall yesterdays ago we never died.

THE MARIONETTES

See how they dream their wooden dreams,
pine legends in their painted eyes.
Their ardor is of crepe and chalk;
the fire is their only surprise.

Catch how they mouth their gargoyle talk;
they even love with a scratching sound.
The fire is their only surprise,
Pinocchio burning himself to the ground.

Watch how they dance their clacking dance;
their kiss is like the breaking of a box.
They would sprout leaves, like fingers of sense —
Master Gepetto, how they dance,

sauntering past with chirping knees
through the proscenium's feast of eyes.
Wanting not to be made of wood,
the fire is their only surprise.

City of iron metaphors,
your children applaud their angular pranks
as their freak noses bump in fiction.
Do they hope that mothers will offer thanks?

See how they turn their necks of bark,
wound and wired for noise and friction.
They are not children lost in the dark.
The fire is their only surprise.

Friend Cricket, like a piccolo,
you weep from the wall your prophecy:

they are so lonely racked on the shelves;
they can weep splinters if only they try.

They're not content to be themselves,
but plot a vegetable sovereignty,
with their sinister, sonorous Italian names
dreaming some varnished mythology.

The fire is their only surprise.
They court the green and yellow courtesan;
in her silver dress she is telling them lies.
The moon is their favorite citizen.

And all unsteadied by their pilgrimage
to this last boondock of a grimy town
visited by their pushcart prompt parades
I spy a hundred wooden strangers in the lemon dawn.

They are shouting I love you in an old dialect,
their chatterbox tarantellas waking the glades-
Colombina, the barking of Melampo,
the toy apples of Giuseppina's breasts,

shimmering forth from the ultimate shores of illusion,
Puncinello, staring with eyes of pearl,
singing I love the child with the blue hair,
I love the green and yellow girl.

HOW I CHANGED MY NAME, FELICE

In Italy a man's name, here a woman's,
transliterated so I went to school
for seven years, and no one told me different.
The teachers hardly cared, and in the class
Italian boys who knew me said Felice,
although outside they called me feh-LEE-tchay.

I might have lived, my noun so neutralized,
another seven years, except one day
I broke a window like nobody's girl,
and the old lady called a cop, whose sass
was wonderful when all the neighbors smiled
and said that there was no boy named Felice.
And then it was it came on me, my shame,
and I stepped up, and told him, and he grinned.

My father paid a quarter for my sin,
called me inside to look up in a book
that Felix was American for me.
A Roman name, I read. And what he said
was that no Roman broke a widow's glass,
and fanned my little neapolitan ass.

A FIG TREE IN AMERICA

They hang full jewel, clusters of ripe figs
on the soft vine, and stir like pregnant women
bothered by a breeze toward new discomforts:
in a keen ache of fullness slowly stir.

August, month of Midas, touches gold
the green branch burgled by the birds and worms
where they hang, in serious attitudes like bombs
in the heaving cockpit of my fierce remembrance:

my father, moving slowly through the ruins,
like Vergil in his baggy overalls,
 to aim his spade as though it were a spear,
and kick, from a cold slum, the slags of Troy.

And here I stand, amid the brick and business,
over the ultimate exile of his grave,
to marvel at my mortal foreigner,
who struck a flag that still can fly so green.

WHO WOULD HAVE THOUGHT

(For Fred Gardaphe)

Who would have thought, I thought,
that gas light in a room
a life ago, would light this poem
my memory has wrought?

It winked across the window panes
of our pocket of a kitchen,
where I without a stitch on,
was being scrubbed for all my stains.
I paddled that dented tub
with angry rub-a-dub dub,
while father mopped the floor
and dared me to spill more.
Then mother wiped my ears,
and sang to dry my tears.
Poor father hummed along;
his voice was much too strong
for such a little ditty,
and more's the pity.

That soap-and-water swimmer
treads shadows in a dream,
though now and then a gleam
of memory casts its shimmer,
like gas light, flicker-fleeter
than skipping rhyme and meter.

FARFALLA

Once, speaking of her brother, Uncle Joe,
my mother mixed the idiom, and put
the foot before the hand in hand-and-foot,
and laughed, and went on talking even so,
about my uncle's zany one-man-show —
a singing waiter on a pleasure boat —
intoning menus with a golden throat,
and dancing three-foot platters heel and toe.

I knew the story, as I also knew
the one he told about my mother too:
how once, far from sun-spattered Italy
a snowflake waltzing down a winter sky
amazed a little girl, who joyfully
sang out then in Italian, "Butterfly!"

ANTONIO STEFANILE
Nola, Italy, 1873-1959

You were a peaceful king, with many spies.
I think of all the slow and careful strangers
walking through the streets of foreign towns
who wore on their watch-chains the gift you sent,
the little coral horn that fought bad luck.
Now you are dead, the lurching continents
seem even less safe than they were before,
so scattered are we — like the Jews, surprised
to our identity this seventh year.
In Argentina children call your name;
who is there left now, old and queer enough
to write, and give advice, and pray for us?
New York and Canada send telegrams,
but where's the Elder now of all our tribe,
the shaman, pipe and proverb, we left home?
Your strength was stubbornness, not luxury:
Anchises turned about, you carried us.
Beyond the sea's walls we remembered Troy,
and you old shade, who stalked that abandoned rubble
like a good shepherd, among sheep of stone.
In Boston an Irish priest trips on your name
to welcome to a world you had not walked
your late reality, your myth that bloomed
like mist beneath that moon of memories,
our banishment. O gentle, antique king,
of spirit large enough for large farewells,
the wind is but a roster of our names
that blow like seeds cast from your ancient earth.

26

CARMEN

(for Daniela Gioseffi)

Carmen, you were seven. You sought me after school,
just came alongside as I marched away,
and fell in stride. I caught your side-long glances.
Beneath your bangs and spit-curls you were pale,
your dark eyes shimmered, you were all eyes.
You talked a blue streak for a stranger,
and I hardly answered. I was shy of words.
You said you were afraid of our old streets,
men shouting at trucks backing in and out
of those huge factory gates, the eerie ring
of cobblestones, as in a spooky movie.
Day after day we walked each other home
to that last corner, where you turned away.
You said you'd cross the street, but I must watch.
I never looked for you except the day
you didn't show up, and I walked home alone.
I wondered if you'd found another friend.
Days later then I heard, while in a store,
holding the bread for mother, you were dead.
There were those women at the spice-laden counter,
saying your name in passing, as at an altar.
I listened in a daze, and looked for mother.
She said that we would stop to light a candle
on the way home at St. Mary-of-the sea.
There at the railing I picked out my candle,
and we said the ten Hail Marys, the Glory Be.
As we walked home my heart raced far ahead,
light-years ahead, I know, to this bright moment,
for now like a godess, stronger than Diptheria,
that godess of dead children, Carmen, you light my mind.

27

ANDREW

Friend, heavy survivor,
you bear the bull's lowered brow,
ready for comers.

To look at you is to understand
jungles are not nice.
My mind creates tableaux

set behind glass — don't touch —
in memory's museum,
especially one of a classroom

and teacher calling you wop.
Or that night in Linden Park
when, head lowered,

you told me your mother was dead.
We were fourteen,
completely uncomforted.

I suppose things are better today.
We are offered courses on dying.
The joggers tell us, Love yourself

Old puff-belly baldhead,
you listen to your kids complain,
and smile.

You make a killing at the track
and zoom home in your huge car,
full of frowns.

For you a proverb might be set:
do not thank the gods too loudly,
or they will hear you and change their minds.

Brother, fellow loser,
I know why in these enlightened times
you still tend the Sacred Heart

on the wall
outside your bedroom
with fragrant candles:

it is the one trophy you understand,
as Jesus taught —
we are all nailed to the wall.

THE DAY WE DANCED THE SAINT
for Zi' Anton'

The day we danced the Saint our shoulders worked
beneath the logs, to the music of a march,
and rowdy with religion we cut loose
to try a jig with that long weight on us,
left flank together, then to the right, then left,
running a little, suddenly stopping dead:
the young girls screamed to watch our statue leap
out of its chocks, it seemed, and lean at them,
his fresh paint flashing in the sun like fire.
The band played *Stella Alpina* and we danced,
red-faced and grinning; grandmothers cackled back
clutching their black shawls, and throwing sweets
wide of the mark, crunched beneath our feet.
Where we pushed on small children ran with us,
skipping and hopping, calling a father's name,
Papa Antonio! like that, in public proof
he held his post beneath the logs that bore
our plaster Saint upon the wooden stage,
where dollars gleamed like sequins on his robe
and made a noise like feathers in the wind.
Next to me Rodolfo puffed and swore,
his face damp with religion and its work,
while up ahead fat Father Ferdinand
swung with the weight, the Pope's own pachyderm,
"*Laetantur coeli!*" roaring to our jibes.
"Don't go to heaven too soon!" Rodolfo cried,
and the logs rumbled, but our Saint stayed put.
I glimpsed my mother peering through the crush,
torn between love of Christ, love of her son,
whose skinny shoulders she feared surely would crack
beneath that holy rubble overhead,

30

but I straightened up, and winked, like some famous athlete,
along with big Arnaldo, Menechin,
Gaetano, Guido, Salvatore and Dino.
We came at last into the smell of wine
and cooking in the air, and the band stopped;
the crowd broke, with a splashing noise, and flags,
shot streamers, colored paper, rained on us,
and suddenly, up front, the old square shone
like a sheet of beaten gold in the noon light.

A young man, like a soldier on report,
raced up to Father Ferdinand, and shouldered
his post with a quick circus-skill that pleased
the elders gathered on the churchyard steps.
The priest walked out, and raised his hands. Shouts back
told him we owned our God that day, at least,
and with a smile he signalled to the women
waiting along the ropes, as at a race,
and they ran to us with glasses, cups and flagons,
streaming along the ranks where we stood firm,
squat, sweating Samsons, holding up our pride.
When my girl found me, as I knew she would,
her fingers thrusting mint-leaves in my mouth
and holding up the wine-flask for my kiss,
I was the purest penitent standing there,
and I dared the forty Saints to break my back.

ATLANTIS

That hunched and crowded town on the eastern coast
blinded the light of the moon with its own moonshine
and held the sea back with a cable line.
Lights technicolor, rust, and rainbow almost,
when these winked out behind me, like a ghost
I toured the night, but I was never lost.

Beyond New Jersey then, I watched hills start
and toil toward mountains, like dark lava rolled
from Alleghany's brimstone red-and-gold
of sunrise, and my eastern heart took heart
to think that the stumbling sea had no such art
to follow where the mountains make a fort.

Then sliding down Ohio's punch-bowl, toward
the Indiana corn-fields, watched them wave;
my new old prairie home made me feel brave.
And never guessed, till now, from what dark hoard
this landlocked moon that blinds me can afford
the light I lost, the sea I never heard.

Landlubber's luck, without a tide to race,
with money in my jeans, hole in my head,
I spy on strangers of squat, farmer's tread,
and wonder, for the years, how many seas
it took to sail their dream to this dry place.

That block of salt, the moon, is good and dead;
those meadows heaving in the summer rain
are not the sea I carry in my head.
I have a different kind of dream to bed,
and wrote this song, and saved my life again.

LETTER FROM A FRIEND IN EXILE

. . . I move among them, neither spy nor slave,
though like a spy I hoard my poverty
and like a slave I count their property
as something strange, and good, and not my own —
for what I touch here, brick, or bark, or bone,
does not touch back the way my fingers felt
the gritty answer of my crumbling hearth
the day I threw my name upon the fire
and ran my nail across the mantel's crack:
(it wandered, like a river on a map.)

But that map's gone, and my lost country gone,
names of cities changed, our temples toppled.
Our children have been herded into pens,
our strong men run away to rocks and caves,
our women tossed like baggage on the shields
of the barbarian. And I am here, in exile,
ghost of a guest to all the gentle hosts.

Ingratitude? No. Thanks are in my heart:
I thank these men for the sound their footsteps make
in the safe night, for their moon's long-legged strut,
their silver Daddy puffing on his pipe
in fifty miles of corn, I thank the dawn
for happening in the sure way it does,
like a fine woman, with her apron gathered,
draping the light's clean clothes on all the lines.
I thank them when I close the door on them,
and hear their voices laughing down the hall,
then fading, as though voices became birds,
and fussed upon the branches, and grew still.

Like eager mutes, the shadows talk to me,
and in the darkness all my shades agree.

But what man needs a friend who will not grieve
when it is time for him to grieve, a friend
who puts his war too soon away from him?
If home is where the heart is, as you say,
then I still burn for my own broken hearth.
You must forgive this, as the sun forgives
the balked raid of the night on your bright fields.

IN THAT FAR COUNTRY

> The clouds are streaming in the sky, like birds.
> The leaves are falling to the ground, like rain.
> My house, unhawsered in the autumn wind,
> Creaks like the ship that took me far from home.
> —*Selma Stefanile*

In that far country formed of coves and bays,
and clouds that float like swans across the sky,
where nothing happens history can praise
or blame, because there is no history,
I read the sun's handwriting on a wall
of ivied hieroglyphs, I spy a town
where the seasons gracefully return and fall
as in a sanctuary all my own.
The language that they speak is greek to me
in that still land. Only the children run;
the women weave their nets besides the sea;
the old men suck their pipes beneath the sun;
and people gather in the village square
to ask about me, why I am not there.

ULISSE, *by Umberto Saba*

Nella mia giovanezza ho navigato
lungo le coste dalmate. Isolotti
a fior d'onda emergevano, ove raro
un ucello sostava intento a prede,
coperti d'alghe, scivolosi, al sole
belli come smeraldi. Quando l'alta
marea e la notte annullava, vele
sottovento sbandavano più al largo
per fuggirne l'insidia. Oggi il mio regno
è quella terra di nessuno. Il porto
accende ad altri i suoi lumi, me al largo
sospinge ancora il non domato spirito,
e della vita il doloroso amore.

UMBERTO SABA: ULYSSES

When I was young I sailed the Dalmatian coast.
Great islands bloomed on the wave; above them flew
once in a while a bird in search of prey.
Covered with kelp, and slippery, under the sun
they shone as beautiful as emeralds.
When night came, and in the high tide they vanished,
with our sails underwind we ducked for the deep
to flee that perilous snare. Today, like that,
my kingdom is No Man's Land. My harbor
burns lanterns for foreigners, and I turn back to sea,
pressed ever on by my unbeaten spirit,
and by my broken-hearted love of life.

translated by Felix Stefanile

37

CECCO ANGIOLIERI (1260?-1313)

Mie madre si m'insegna medicina
la qual non m'è crudelmente, sana:
che' mmi dice ch'i' usi a la campana
da otto pesche o diece la mattina,

che mmi faran campar de la contina
e di febbre quartan' e di terzana;
molto mi loda l'anguille di chiana,
che ' l cap' e me' ch' otriaca fina.

Carne di bu' e cascio e cipolle
molte me loda, quand'i' sento doglia,
e ch'i' ne faccia ben buona satolla;

e se di questo non avessi voglia,
e stessi quasimente su la colla,
molto mi loda porri con le foglia.

CECCO COMPLAINS ABOUT HIS
MOTHER'S CURE-ALL

(For Paolo Giordano)

My mother brings me up on medicine
that sad to tell does not agree with me,
though with the morning bells I dutifully
choke down her breakfast of eight pears or ten,

to keep the plague away, and hex, and pain,
the fever of the four days or the three.
Alas, with me, I find that eels agree:
one eel is worth all cures that famish men.

And I find beef, and cheese, and onions too,
they really go down well when I feel bad;
with such a bellyful I can make do.

But when recuperation can't be had,
and my prognosis is, at best, quite sad,
I mix them up with greens, and make a stew.

translated by Felix Stefanile

ON A REMARK BY THE POET,
DANA GIOIA, ON TRANSLATING

> Translation is inevitable, in the first place,
> because of the curse of Babel. . .
> —*Robert M. Adams*

It is sheer coveting, that much is clear,
of someone else's folly and surprise,
and soothes your secret fever as you peer
into another person's heart, to see
with calm, untroubled eyes,
how things may be and how things may not be.
The act of a voyeur,
you spy a fellow out, and take his lies
for granted, your own motives less than pure.
Then you fix his measure, take a look
in a strange dictionary, and try your luck.

Out of the poem you gingerly extract
the live-coal from the clinker in the grate;
then envy glosses into cunning tact,
the shimmering in your hands. By fits and starts
you ponder, study, weigh, you extricate
from gritty clots the gleaming private parts.
Soon it's like keeping score;
your pencil flails away, moods don't distract,
and the grisly business leaves no trace of gore.
When you are finished, watch him strut and rage;
it isn't you that's crying in the cage.

This will not do for Homer, you've been told,
or Dante. Shakespeare has the best of it
for changing englished Plutarch into gold.
That wasn't alchemy, but outright theft.

40

No doubt our mother wit
does well enough — though we are all bereft
since Babel's shame —
to strike a phrase cast from our own stronghold,
but you're translating now, so stake your claim —
we're babbling foreigners all, and none the worse
for Bibles put to native prose and verse.

THE DANCE AT ST. GABRIEL'S

for Louis Otto

We were the smart kids of the neighborhood
where, after high school, no one went to school,
you NYU and I CCNY.
We eyed each other at St. Gabriel's
on Friday nights, and eyed each other's girls.
You were the cute, proverbial good catch
— just think of it, nineteen — and so was I,
but all we had was moonlight on our minds.
This made us cagey; we would meet outside
to figure how to dump our dates, go cruising.
In those hag-ridden and race-conscious times
we wanted to be known as anti-fascists,
and thus get over our Italian names.
When the war came, you volunteered, while I
backed in by not applying for deferment,
for which my loving family named me Fool.
Once, furloughs overlapping, we met up,
the Flight Lieutenant and the PFC;
we joked about the pair we made, and sauntered.
That Father Murray took one look at us,
and said our Air Force wings were the only wings
we'd ever earn. We lofted up our beers.
Ah, Louis, what good times we two have missed.
Your first time up and out the Germans had you,
and for your golden wings they blew you down.

SOLDIERS AND THEIR GIRLS

(First Three-Day Pass)

Those years before Fast Food a pizza meant
a neighborhood, an accent maybe, or
the way the customers looked. You had your limits.
One train-stop more it might be Fish and Chips,

or Blintzes. What a way to spend a date,
skipping from joint to joint, and getting drunk
on laughter and strange sipping, stupid jokes
about the squid, rose-water, or flat-bread.

Whatever, down it went. You smiled and smiled
because the girl was pretty and proud
and scared. She wanted you to know
Armenians were just like you, or Jews,

and we were all Americans anyway.
You checked your watch, said "Hitler!" She teared up,
pert Rosie Ohanessian, whose large eyes
were darker than that last night on your mind.

She walked you to the depot. You held hands,
but never made a move, the station crammed,
young couples slouching, grinning, waiting for
the speaker to announce the bus from camp.

BALLAD OF THE WAR BRIDE

Willie, on leave, got married, and came home
to show his discharge, and show off his bride,
a gangling, giggling girl from Birmingham
without a cent. His mother almost died.

His father came right out and talked expense,
and told them that this wasn't Alabam.
The kids agreed. As if doing penance
they both found jobs, and soon the money came.

His mother grumbled on, as did his father;
they said they couldn't understand her speech.
A girl with yellow hair was too much bother,
and they were sure that she was using bleach.

One day they told him, fever in their eyes,
"Kick in more money, and we'll save for you."
Then it was that Willie, past surprise,
knew what he and his sweetheart had to do.

One morning, trim deportment a pure sham,
they left for work as far as one could tell,
but with train tickets back to Birmingham.
He called his folks en route, and told them go to hell.

HONORABLE ARMY DISCHARGE

My heart was full of money, and my head
was full of dreams, the day that I got home
for good. My mother cried and cried, my sisters
cried; my brother, turned fourteen, just stared
and laughed, and stuck his finger to his head
and rolled his eyes. It was as if to say
that things were back to normal now, and crazy.

When Pop came home from work, harroomph, harroomph,
he asked me if I'd been to see my room,
the new paint job. He tripped upon a word,
said something about a new bloom sweeping clean.

That broke things up, we laughed, we all sat down
to eat and talk. I choked the pasta down
as best I could; it was so rich and sweet,
the taste of a largesse I had forgotten.
I never guessed at yearning, those lost years,
until late in the night. The new paint job
seared through my nostrils, and brought out the tears,
my room so small, so safe, so quiet I heard
the drumming in my ears, my heart's own cannon
time and again go whoosh and whoosh and thud.

BACK HOME IN INDIANA

I get home,
like Charlie Chaplin,
all my dirigibles floating.

Gimpy from work
I sit, and drink, and think
there is much sailing to be done in Indiana —
at least one good ocean to dig,
some seventy thousand sea-gulls to be imported
and the right kind of foreigner, the wrong kind,
with black hair, gold teeth and a lucky parrot.

Across the Wabash one day
I'd heard Mexican field-hands, their delicate noise:
real Indians in Tippecanoe County,
right next to the Methodist Church.

Montauk! Montauk!
I cried, in my mind's leap,
thinking of that last page
in *The Great Gatsby* —
the homeless shore,
naked, unnamed,
the dunes of Long Island swirled like carpets
ready for the tread of Europe.

And here, in the central plain, the final result:
history, a cleared table;
corn, heaped up like bullion, like the cross-over vote.
Safe from the pull of the tide and the smell of the moon
there is no rocking the boat in Indiana.

TO BE FRANK ABOUT IT

(For Anthony J. Tamburri)

Lord of the loser, and the truant's god,
a hellbent high school dropout fast for ruin,
he didn't end up shining shoes. Instead,
Fame licked his boots, and women licked their lips.
Saints walk through walls. Sinatra was no saint,
and yet he soared through ceilings like a wisp,
the electronic angel of an age,
on wings of song, despite the smoker's cough.
The cleaned out gambler, the receptionist
who falls in love each time a dream walks in
and puts his briefcase down, and smiles at her,
the cousins from Hoboken pray to him.
Now he has vanished, old time columnists
punch their computers blind to find the words
to put him down, the magic and the madness
that summoned armies. Envy stares, aghast,
to think this swaggering, crass evangelist
who came from cobbled streets and cold room flats
should sing of heaven where no heaven was,
in Babylon and Hollywood and home,
the place where such thoughts last. There some young girl,
some old coot who is kicking off his shoes
to clear his head, is listening to the songs.
It is the jaunty fox who now must weep,
and weep the longest. If Audacity
goes down, what shall we tell the little ones
of courage and persistence, and the hunt
that keeps them hungry and that keeps them fed?

Taking Sides with John Ciardi

—some words on minus-American poetry

When Robert Lowell hyphenated you —
Italian, hyphen sign, American —
to praise your poetry, your answer ran
in rough-house expletives. Your passion flew,
and subsequently in an interview
you squelched his harmless seeming little hyphen
as not the way to write out citizen.
How culture-vultures smiled at the to-do.

If this is poetry, as may be true,
it's also punctuation, not too thin
a point or line for morals that you drew.
We all know grammar can stick like a pin,
and those who think my point is overdrawn,
they are no friends of yours, nor of mine, John.

A Poem for Selma

Water dripping: the insatiable voice
of the radio, sarcastic bee
buzzing through the cheap sunlight of our rooms;
the hall, dark as a warehouse, and our clothes
slumped over chairs, in silent, dreadful poses,
crumpled flags
slipped in a sudden ambush; piles of books
scattered, as slate torn in the morning wind
of our hurry — all, all our choice and chattel,
and we make for it, each night, from the long train
dumping us, like troops, to a dim outpost
in the domestic jungle of our lives.

That grouch, my shadow, waylays every move
she makes, for booby-traps galore
flickering under touch: the pillows staled;
papers, like clues, under the bed; cracked combs
her fingers cannot heal,
and the smell of a crazy kitchen
where she burns to know the woman that she is.

Canned goods, in rhymes of color, stacked on shelves,
remember landscapes dreamed unleft
in the lucky midnight when our sleep was sound.
The clock, like rivers, flowed. The alley dripped
Babylon, and the rain fell —
moss on the wall, and mushrooms in the brick.

There is conspiracy in all these smells:
pine in the soap and talcum in the bleach,
whore's air of roses in the insecticide,
all the expensive junk of cleanliness.

The ugliness of this poem is my love:
I think how even the germs are frightened by it.

Outside, a code of spectrums on the street
holy my prison with the prism's soul.
I remember that morning waking, dizzily floating,
thrashing through swirling sheets toward reality's mud,
a paper-swimmer, tearing on the rocks of morning.

I tugged at the fur
of my long beast dream,
but the dog's nose was cold.

I staggered toward linoleum reefs
where my sun was, shining
in rich, aluminum stripes
on the radiator.

And then you woke, in that iron-colored air,
saying, It's time, not, as I ask,
Is it time?
In the distance, over the rusty shacks of the morning,
that crooked map shaped in reliefs of gravel,
we heard a rooster crying impossibly,
and he was saying Peacock, Peacock, Peacock.

EMILY

Should mortal lips divine
The undeveloped freight
Of a delivered syllable
'T would crumble with the weight.
    —*Emily Dickinson*

We know that Emily would place a finger
upon a letter in a word, and linger,
lost in imagination's curlicues,
because a friend had sent her pretty news.

Words, the syllables, the sounds, the grace
of penmanship, or how lines danced with space
across a page, it was to catch their gist
she peered and peered, merry cabalist.

She once confessed she kept herself away
from opening an envelope all day
to read the vision her denial spun.
Anticipation warmed her like the sun.

Spry angel, safe in heaven, when upstairs,
but kitchen heretic, she put on airs
and thought of poems while baking father's cake.
The light through the window slanted for her sake.

Merry and naught, and gay and numb, she wrote
about herself. She had the antidote:
she tracked the moth beneath the metaphor;
then East and West, like hinges, swung a door.

Coy hymnodist, who rarely went to church,
her meter never left her in the lurch.

As for the tunes, Revival cast its moods,
and her piano echoed through the woods.

She cobbled up her verse on scraps of paper;
how they ignited from her flickering taper —
a gleaming galaxy of joy and doubt,
some worlds put in, and some worlds put to rout.

She stitched the scraps of paper into sheaves,
and pressed them down, like folded handkerchiefs,
into a chest her father never saw.
Ah, what a dowry for the Bride of Awe!

Some she mailed out, as pert as valentines,
to friends and relatives. Like ore in mines
they hid in attics, albums, cellar murk,
until uncovered by the digger's work.

I praise these archeologists of craft
who piece shards together she had left,
the daft and deft designs, the blinding jewel
tucked in the folds of an old, forgotten shawl.

Old Untermeyer, in his anthology,
said neighbors thought her but an oddity.
She had the great misfortune, and the will,
to be — unlike her neighbors — original.

Now scholars, out to get her with their praises,
bedeck her with their own outlandish phrases.
One well meant term for her is "heroinism,"
but Emily was her own neologism.

She stays, the mistress of her mystery,
despite our good intentions: Emily,
who said, "My business is Circumference,"
still wore her skin around her like a fence.

Ah, Emily, forgive our late respect:
Americans are never circumspect.
We shower you with our own mad surprise;
you disappeared before our very eyes.

Forgive me too, who make a clumsy case.
I've borrowed from you, and purloined your grace.
Forgive me, if you can, sad Muse, my small gray dove,
for my presumption, but not for my love.

HUBIE

Army experiments with mixed units:
Negroes being admitted into white
companies. —
           News Item 1943

You, Hubie, were the one and only black
in our whole crazy outfit. You had a knack
for fending off our clumsy comradeship.
You were a ferret at a Freudian slip
or condescension: (let's ask Hubie, too!)
You always answered, "Cut it out, will you?"
Except one time: the night we made to go
to the Anselmo Club, and wouldn't you know,
we challenged you, we forced you, kidnapped you
to come along. You came. We wrecked the place.
The frightened 4F doorman mentioned race,
held his hand up to his pasty face,
and said you had no card, no "membership."
He tried to close the door; Paul knocked his grip,
and hollered, "He's our guest!" Then the poor guy said No,
and Paul, half drunk already, just let go.
That was a fight we all enjoyed but you;
the cops came, and your black skin saved our hides,
because the owner blamelessly denied
that there was trouble, and we made no news.
No news was good for him, and good for us,
but the drink you drank that night was bitter, bitter juice.

Then there was Captain Jones from Millidgeville
(Gee-AY!) who hated you so hard it killed
to hear him give you his Boy-this, Boy-that.
He hated all of us, but that was pure so what
to the dockside bruisers, city toughs,

and all the ill-assorted country roughs
that made up our sad clan of prison-chasers:
we knew that you were the true King of Losers.
Maybe that's why we liked you, let that stay,
from ignorance to shame to light of day.
Jones ran us like a chain-gang, that's for sure,
but your bland moon-face shone, "Endure, endure."

Once I glimpsed you with the Enemies.
It was their singing time. They were a breeze
to guard, no trouble. It was a heavy night
of stars and blooms, of shadows that turned bright.
A kid cupped his right hand up to his face
the way they did to magnify the voice,
and winked at you. Hubie, you winked back.
It was a sign between you for a song,
and then he gave their yodel, loud and long,
fronni e limoni, which maybe signified
some legend lost when ancient glory died,
but left its echo. No one would begin
before the signal, *lemon leaves*, had run
in gross annunciation. The same phrase
would introduce each stanza. In a daze
I heard the eerie music, though this time
the voice I heard was yours, in Neapolitan rhyme,
and my translation of it is a crime:

Oh leaves of the lemon trees! It's in the shape of crosses
they are constructed, all the gates of prison,
the better to destroy the sons of mothers.
Ah, Hubie, what a maundering in my heart
to hear you go falsetto, sob and start,
and grace-note the muezzin-vaunt of words,
gliding the vowels over, like slow birds,
the drawn out line. I thought my head would burst.
For their lament those lads made you sing first;
you knew the chant; it could have been the blues,
three lines of heartbreak, blood down to your shoes.

Then came the answers, in the same old notes,
one fellow, then another, golden throats —
tears for a mother, or a girl back home,
some nasty verse on the Pope in Rome,
and when your turn came round again you sang
about the way the bells of Nola rang.
Mad Captain Jones's "damn eye-talian crew"
had caught your grave compassion, trusted you,
and taught you more Italian for a song
than the rest of us had learned the whole year long.
Those distant bells, they did you no more good,
than did the chimes of elegant Englewood,
New Jersey, where you came from, preacher's son,
out of a tiny Baptist congregation
made up of cooks and gardeners, garbage men,
and other service people all hemmed in.
The war came, you were ready, just like me,
which meant no job, no future, and no money.

What now comes back to me, old Hubie, is
how you and I could sit and shoot the breeze
those Sunday afternoons, when things went dead
in repple-depple camp. The peace went to my head.
We chuckled about week-end roll-calls, played
the same each muster: mostly no one up
except us cowards who were thin on hope,
afraid to miss the check and rate KP,
although in truth half our company
slept through. The guys took turns as stand-ins, one
for every two or three in mock attention,
answering for O'Toole or Policetti
or Garbatino. Sergeant Parmelee
stared straight down at his pad, and called the lot,
then swung around to go back to his cot.
"Why don't you slack off, Hubie?" I asked once.
You snorted, as though you took me for a dunce,
patted my knee with that ham hand of yours,
and said, "Because for me it would just be my arse.

56

With my complexion can't you see the fun?"
The simple truth fell on me like a ton.

Poor twins, we were discharged on the same day,
a lot to do, pick up our pay,
strip down our cots — "They might just change their minds,"
our sergeant snarled, "so move your fat behinds" —
sweep out the years, go listen to the lecture
on Re-enlistment and Reserve, some double feature;
then scoot to chow, and back to Camp Supply.

The Quartermaster goof-off, Sleepy Eye,
just brushed our gear aside, and made us sign.
On our way out we passed a clothing bin;
talk about brave! I knew we were civilians
when I snitched a cap, an Eisenhower jacket,
and so did you, you bum, and you said, "Fuck it."
The whole platoon was gone when we got back,
the silence of the barracks pure whip-crack
of memories in my head, I stared at you.
You said, "There's still one thing for us to do,"
and handed me a sheet, hodge-podge
of name, address, and Bible verse for pledge
all loyalty, no betrayal. To make things worse
I read aloud that thundering, crying verse,
because you told me once I was a poet.
What boobs we were; how kind we didn't know it.
I handed you a map of streets, instructions,
accompanied by four-letter imprecations
of what would happen if you didn't write me,
or come and visit. Then you'd have to fight me.
The map showed names of streets and bus route numbers.
All at once we stopped. We were struck dumb.
You blinked your eyes, and made a choking noise.
That was enough for me; I lost my voice.

We neither of us wrote. What came
between? It was not a forgetting. It was time
that took its aim, and brought us down like fools.
We had survived — according to the rules —
the deaths, the separations, all the cant
of war, of honor, and the special rant
of patriotism. We had saved our skins
through years of soldiering, the tightrope dance
of danger, boredom, whatever we fought for;
ourselves, we knew, were the true spoils of war.
We moved from that into the orgy of
the personal release of pure self-love.

The time is gone for what we should have said
or done, old Hubie. All the dead are dead.
Time was once ripe. Now time's a rotten thought.
Yet blow me down, and scratch me for an ought,
we buddied to the end, just to endure.
(There is a thought here that is less than pure.)

A black man and a white man, that's for sure,
this other war, and the cagey cowardice
of habit, turning honest blood to ice.
I think that we were brothers once, "The Twins,"
the fellows called us, masking their wide grins.
What's left is poetry, the penance for my sins.

The Americanization of the Immigrant

Your words, Genoveffa,
through the open window,
telling me once again
what to buy at the store —
don't forget, don't forget —
aroma of fresh bread
almost a halo.

That was a long time ago.
I never forgot.
Like Dante
I have pondered and pondered
the speech I was born to,
lost now, mother gone,
the whole neighborhood bull-dozed,
and no one to say it on the TV,
that words are dreams.

ABOUT THE AUTHOR

Felix Stefanile was born in 1920 in Long Island City, New York. He was educated in the public schools and at CCNY. A World War II veteran, he found employment after the war in a series of clerical jobs until 1950, when he began his eleven-year stint in the New York State Department of Labor. There he eventually became a middle functionary in worker's claims and entitlements. In 1954 he and his wife Selma started the poetry magazine *Sparrow*, which is now one of the oldest poetry journals in the United States. His essay, "The Imagination of the Amateur," which expresses his ideas on independent literary publishing in American history was published in 1966. The essay gained him a National Endowment for the Arts Prize in 1967, and has been anthologized.

In 1961, Felix Stefanile was invited by Purdue University to serve as Visiting Poet and Lecturer for one year. At the end of his tenure, the university asked him to stay on as a member of the English faculty. He taught freshman composition, survey courses, and a Poetry Writing class that drew campus-wide attention. In 1969 he was appointed to a Full Professorship, and in 1973 was awarded the Standard Oil of Indiana Prize for Best Teacher. His poetry awards include the Emily Clark Balch Prize of the *Virginia Quarterly Review* in 1972. In 1997 he was the first recipient of the recently established John Ciardi Award for life-long achievement in Italian American poetry.

PINO APRILE, *Terroni: All That Has Been Done to Ensure That the Italians of the South Become "Southerners,"* Vol. 72, Ethnic/Cultural Studies, $20

EMANUEL DI PASQUALE, *Harvest,* Vol. 71, Poetry, $10

ROBERT ZWEIG, *Return to Naples,* Vol. 70, Memoir, $16

LETIZIA AIROS AND OTTORINO CAPELLI, EDS., *Guido,* Vol. 69, Italian/American Studies, $12

FRED GARAPHÉ, *Moustche Pete Is Dead! Evviva Baffo Pietro! The* Fra Noi *Columns 1985–19855,* Vol. 67, Literature/Oral History, $12

PAOLO RUFFILLI, *Dark Room,* Vol. 66, Poetry, $10

HELEN BAROLINI, *Crossing the Alps,* Vol. 65, Fiction, $14

COSMO FERRARA, *Profiles of Italian Americans,* Vol. 64, Italian/American Studies, $16

GIL FAGIANI, *Chianti in Connecticut,* Vol. 63, Poetry, $10

PIERO BASSETTI, NICCOLÓ D'AQUINO, *Italic Lessons,* Vol. 62, Italian/American Studies $10

GRACE CAVALIERI AND SABINE PASCARELLI, EDS., *The Poet's Cookbook,* Vol. 61, Poetry/Recipes, $12

EMANUEL DI PASQUALE, *Siciliana,* Vol. 60, Poetry, $8

NATALIA COSTA-ZALESSOW, ED., JOAN E. BORRELLI, TRANSLATOR, *Francesca Turini Bufalini: Autobiographical Poems,* Vol. 59, Poetry, $18

RICHARD VETERE, *Baroque,* Vol. 58, Fiction, $18

LEWIS PUTNAM TURCO, *La Famiglia / The Family,* Vol. 57, Memoir, $15

NICK JAMES MILETI, *The Unscrupulous: Scams, Cons, Fakes, and Fraud That Poison the Fine Arts,* Vol. 56, Humanities, $20

PIERO BASSETTI, PAOLINO ACCOLLA, NICCOLO D'AQUINO, *Italici: An Encounter with Bassetti,* Vol. 55, Italian Studies, $8

GIOSE RIMANELLI, *The Three-Legged One,* Vol. 54, Fiction, $15

CHARLES KLOPP, *Bele Antiche Storie,* Vol. 53, Critiscism, $25

JOSEPH RICAPITO, *Second Wave,* Vol. 52, Poetry, $12

GARY R. MORMINO, *Italians in Florida,* Vol. 51, Italiana Americana/History, $15

GIANFRANCO ANGELUCCI, GIUSEPPE NATALE, TRANSLATOR, *Federico F,* Vol. 50, Fiction, $16

ANTHONY VALERIO, *The Little Sailor,* Vol. 49, Fiction, $8. **OUT OF PRINT**

ROSS TALARICO, *The Reptilian Interludes,* Vol. 48, Poetry, $15

RACHAEL GUIDO DEVRIES, *Teeny Tiny Tino's Fishing Story,* Vol. 47, Children's Literature, $6

EMANUEL DI PASQUALE, *Writing Anew: New and Selected Poems,* Vol. 46, Poetry, $15

MARIA FAMA, *Looking for Cover,* Vol. 45, Poetry, $15

ANTHONY VALERIO, *Toni Cade Bambara's One Sicilian Night,* Vol. 44, Memoir, $44. **OUT OF PRINT**

EMANUEL CARNEVALI, DENNIS BARONE, ED., *Furnished Rooms,* Vol. 43, Poetry, $14

Published by Bordighera, Inc., an independently owned not-for-profit scholarly organization
that has no legal affiliation to the University of Florida, the John D. Calandra Italian Amer-
ican Institute, or State University of New York at Stony Brook.